my
JEWISH
FAITH

About this book

The titles in the *My Faith* collection are designed to introduce young children to the six world faiths and each focuses on a child and his or her family from a particular faith community. Whilst the approach and the language level are appropriate for young readers, some of the key concepts will need to be supported by sensitive clarification by an adult. The *Notes for Teachers and Parents* on pages 4 and 5 provide extra information to help develop children's knowledge and understanding of the different beliefs and traditions.

VISIT OUR WEBSITE www.evansbooks.co.uk

First published in this edition in 2006 by
Evans Brothers Limited
2A Portman Mansions
Chiltern St
London W1U 6NR

Printed in China by WKT Company Limited

British Library Cataloguing in Publication Data

Clark, Anne, 1949-
    My Jewish faith. - (My Faith)
    1. Judaism - Juvenile literature 2. Jewish children - Religious life - Juvenile literature
    3. Jews - Juvenile literature
    I. Title
    296
    ISBN 0237531755
    13 digit ISBN (from 1 January 2007) 9780237 53175 1

Editor: Su Swallow
Design: D.R. ink
Production: Jenny Mulvanny
Reading consultant: Lesley Clark, Reading and Language Information Centre
Series consultant: Alison Seaman, The National Society's Religious Education Centre
Commissioned photography: David Rose

Acknowledgements
The author would like to thank Zoë Baum and her family; Rabbi Menachem Junik and the members of the Richmond Synagogue; Jacob Colton; the Citron family. The author would also like to thank Clive Lawton for his helpful comments on the manuscript and John Trotter/Manor House Books for the loan of religious articles. Due to certain requirements of Jewish law, some of the situations shown here were specially created for this book.

For permission to reproduce copyright material the author and publishers gratefully acknowledge the following: pages 13, 14, 15, 24 David Rose; page 28 B&G Balhetchet/Quality Photography; page 29 Philip Baum

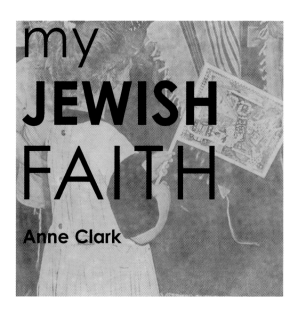

my
JEWISH
FAITH

Anne Clark

Contents

Evans

Notes for Teachers and Parents

Pages 6/7 Jews believe in One God, the Creator of the Universe, who is also a personal God. The Torah, which was revealed by God to Moses on Mount Sinai, contains the central teachings of Judaism. Jews serve God by carrying out the laws contained in the Torah; belief in God has to be complemented by righteous actions. There are some 13.5 million Jews in the world today, of whom just under 300,000 live in the UK. Jews see themselves as an extended family, rather than a race or a religion. Family life is of key importance in the transmission of Jewish traditions and values.

Pages 8/9 Observant Jews do not work or travel on Shabbat, which is a day set aside for spiritual renewal and family life. On Friday evening family and friends gather at home for a special meal. The two special loaves of bread, called challah (pronounced hallah) represent the double portion of manna which God provided for the Israelites in the wilderness on the eve of Shabbat and festivals, (see Exodus 16: 22/26).

Pages 10/11 Shabbat ends at nightfall on Saturday with a ceremony called havdalah, meaning separation. Lighting the plaited havdalah candle is the first act of work after Shabbat. The overflowing cup of wine is a symbol of joy. The spices symbolize the 'sweetness' of Shabbat which Jews wish to take with them into the working week. The play of light and shadow on the cupped hands held out towards the candle flame is a symbolic parallel of the distinction between Shabbat and the weekdays.

Pages 12/13 Zoe's family worships in an Orthodox synagogue in which men and women sit separately. The males cover their head with a kippah (skullcap) as a sign of respect for God and wear a tallit or prayer shawl. Married women are also required to cover their hair. The Ark, which is the cupboard containing the Torah scrolls, is at the front of the synagogue and is generally only opened to remove or return a scroll.

Pages 14/15 The Torah scroll is handwritten by a trained scribe on parchment made from the skins of kosher animals. Both photos show boys celebrating their Bar Mitzvah (a Jewish boy's coming of age at 13 years old), one in London, the other at the Western Wall in Jerusalem. This is all that remains of the Temple today and is a place of prayer and pilgrimage for Jewish people.

Pages 16/17 The mezuzah is a small handwritten parchment scroll containing the declaration of basic Jewish beliefs. It is rolled up, placed in a protective case and fixed to the right-hand doorpost of every room in Jewish homes, synagogues and shops, except the bathroom and toilet, in response to the command: 'you shall write them (these words) on doorposts of your house' (Deuteronomy 6 : 9).

Pages 18/19 Many children who do not go to Jewish schools attend supplementary classes which are generally held in the synagogue on Sunday mornings. The curriculum includes the study of Hebrew, Torah, Jewish history, customs and celebrations. The children also learn about the mitzvot or commandments (singular mitzvah) which Jews are expected to fulfil, such as Tzedaka, the obligation to give to people in need. The Hebrew writing on Zoe's money box says Tzedaka.

Pages 20/21 The main celebration of the festival of Pesach is the seder meal when the story of the Exodus from Egypt is read from a book called the hagadah. The seder was designed as an educational experience for children. Zoe can be seen asking four questions about the seder, traditionally the role of the youngest child present. The seder plate contains symbolic foods, such as a roast egg and roast bone. Zoe and her father are dipping bitter herbs (horseradish) symbolizing the bitterness of slavery into a sweet paste called haroset. Notice the beautifully embroidered cloth covering the unleavened bread or matzah.

Pages 22/23 The basic regulations about kosher food are laid down in Leviticus 11 with regard to the animals, birds and fish that Jews are permitted to eat. In addition, animals and birds must be killed by a prescribed painless method and the blood removed. Jews are not allowed to eat meat and dairy foods at the same meal.

Pages 24/25 Sukkot is a time of thanksgiving for food and for shelter. The sukkah calls to mind the temporary dwellings used by the Israelites while wandering in the wilderness. The most important part of the structure is the roof which is made of cut branches and must be open to the sky. Children enjoy decorating the sukkah with fruit and with their own artwork. Simchat Torah is the festival at the end of Sukkot when Jews celebrate the completion and immediate recommencement of the annual cycle of Torah readings in the synagogue.

Pages 26/27 Hanukkah commemorates the deliverance of the Jews from religious persecution in the 2nd century BCE and the subsequent rededication of the Temple in Jerusalem. It is celebrated by lighting oil lamps or candles, one light on the first night, two the second and so on up to eight. Presents are exchanged and there are special Hanukkah foods and games. Jewish people light a yahrzeit or memorial candle each year on the anniversary of the death of close relatives. The candle burns for 24 hours and symbolizes the departed soul.

Pages 28/29 Jewish couples get married under a canopy called a huppah (pronounced hoo-pa) which symbolizes the Jewish home which they will build together. The canopy is often decorated with flowers. Baby boys receive their Jewish names when they are circumcised at eight days of age. In Orthodox communities girls are given their Jewish names when the father recites a blessing in the synagogue on the Shabbat following their birth. In progressive communities, both boys and girls have a naming ceremony in the synagogue on a Shabbat morning.

Hello! My name is Zoë.

My family
and I are
Jewish.
Jews believe
in one God
who is the
Creator of
the world.
God cares
for everyone.

Every Friday evening we celebrate
the start of **Shabbat**. Shabbat is a
day of rest, fun and prayer for
Jewish people.

How do you celebrate?

We light candles. We drink wine and share sweet white bread.

It lasts until Saturday night. At the end of Shabbat we light another candle and smell sweet spices.

We hold our
hands towards
the candle
and feel the
warmth of
the flame.

Where do Jews meet for worship?

We go to synagogue to pray to God together with our family and friends. We go on Shabbat and on festival days.

Who is this?

This is the **rabbi**, the leader of our Jewish community. He is holding one of the **Torah** scrolls.

What is a Torah scroll?

A Torah scroll contains the first five books of the Bible. It is written in Hebrew, the language Jewish people use for worship.

This Torah scroll is in Jerusalem, in Israel. Jerusalem is a special place for Jewish people.

What is this tiny scroll called?

It is a mezuzah. It contains words from the Torah. It is kept in a small case.

Jewish people put a mezuzah on doorposts in their house. Some Jews touch it as they go in and out of their home.

We go to Sunday classes to learn how to live as a Jew.

Jews have to help people in need. I help by giving some money each week. I put the money in a special box.

What is your favourite festival?

I like **Pesach**, because all my family are together for a special meal called the **seder**.

What are you doing here?

We eat special foods to help us tell the story of how God freed the Jews from Egypt long ago.

What kinds of food do Jews eat?

The Torah tells us what foods we can eat and how to cook them. These foods are called kosher.

At **Rosh Hashanah**, we eat slices of apple dipped in honey.

We pray for a sweet and happy new year.

During the week of **Sukkot**, we eat all our meals outside in a hut called a sukkah.

On Simchat Torah we sing and dance with the Torah scrolls to show how happy we are to have the Torah.

Tonight is the sixth night of **Hanukkah.** We light an extra candle on our **hanukiah** on each of the eight nights of the festival.

My grandparents light a special candle each year to remember their parents on the day that they died.

What about the happy times in your family?

Jewish people like to celebrate together. I was a bridesmaid at my cousin's wedding. She married in a synagogue.

This is my
cousin's baby.
It is his naming
ceremony.
We all said a
special prayer
to welcome him
into the Jewish
community.

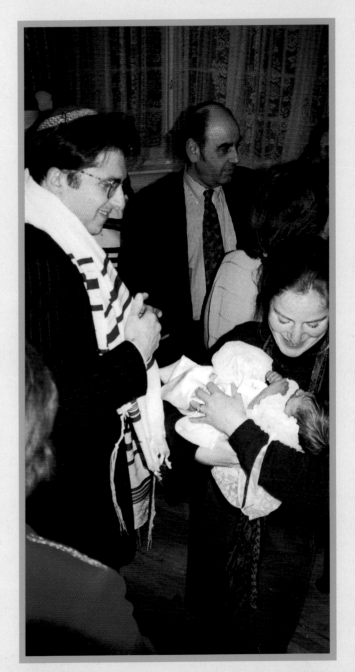

Glossary

hanukiah - A lamp with nine branches used during Hanukkah.

Hanukkah - A festival of lights.

Pesach - A spring festival when Jews remember their escape from slavery in Egypt.

rabbi - A Jewish religious teacher and leader.

Rosh Hashanah - The Jewish New Year.

seder - A special meal in Jewish homes on Pesach.

Shabbat - The Jewish day of rest and celebration which lasts from sunset on Friday until nightfall on Saturday.

Sukkot - An autumn harvest festival.

Torah - The first five books of the Bible.

Index